MEMORIES
OF
PINECREST

Dedication

In Memoriam:

To my Mom and Dad

MEMORIES OF PINECREST

Patrick A. Taylor

Edited and Proofed by Robert Cooper and Laurie Hood

Published by Taylor Press, Placerville, CA

Please visit my website at www.pinecrestlake.net

Copyright © 2006 by Patrick A. Taylor

All rights reserved. No part of this book may be reproduced or transmitted in any form or by any means, electronic or mechanical, including photocopying, recording, or by any information storage and retrieval system, without permission in writing from the author or publisher.

Printed by Pacific Copy and Print, Sacramento, CA.

ISBN-10 0-9789240-0-2
ISBN-13 978-09789240-0-3

First Edition

<u>Acknowledgements</u>

I wish to thank the following people for helping make this book possible.

My wife, Mayda, for understanding why I stayed up so late and devoted more time to this book than I did her, and for not questioning why I received so many e-mails from former girlfriends.

To my neighbor and friend Robert C., for his literary expertise and daily sandwiches.

To Linda J., Sheila H., Nancy B., Sandra C., Joan Y., Karen K., Linda T., and Norm S. (how did he get in there?) and everyone else that contributed remembrances.

Table of Contents

Preface

It is my hope that you, the reader, will enjoy reading this book as much as I enjoyed writing it.

It has taken over 24 years of research to complete. True, 21 of those years were spent living life while only 3 years were actually spent in its compellation. It is a non-fiction work whose sole purpose is not only to inform and entertain, but also to make one probe into the recesses of their mind for the happiest moments in their youth. It is a means of escape. It is hoped that it will bring back memories to the reader that have long been suppressed.

While this book is about experiences in a small resort area located on the western slopes of the Sierra Nevada mountain range in California, it could be any location across the globe where youth comes of age.

"Did everything you wrote about really happen as you say it did?"; "What you remember of Pinecrest is not what I remember". These are questions and comments that were posted in the guest book on my website during the writing and research of this book.

Why is it then, that two (or more) people can experience the same event at the same time, or for that matter similar events in the same environment, even at different times, and have different recollections of what actually took place? Or maybe didn't take place? Confusing? Read on...

There has been a plethora of research on the subject of memory fluctuations and loss. One such explanation might be the natural process of aging and decay of the brain, known as "transience". Another might be "misattribution", which is believing you have seen something you haven't. Yet another might be "suggestibility", which is the incorporation of misinformation into memory due to leading questions, deception, or other causes. Even "absent-mindedness", which usually occurs when so many things are happening at once, that your main focus prevents you from giving the proper attention to everything else. It makes you give second thoughts to the benefits of "multi-tasking", which may be beneficial to computers, but may have detrimental effects in humans. In my case, I think I am experiencing all of these symptoms at once!

Now that we completely understand what it is I am trying to say, or what I didn't say but meant to if I remember correctly, we must move on to a time and place that exists, or at least used to exist not only in our minds but in actuality as well. I think.

I had one reader remark that "Pinecrest is magical. It is timeless. It is the one last place on earth where summer love still comes true generation after generation". Perhaps I was under a misconception that the Pinecrest of today does not hold the "magical allure" that was so apparent in the past. It appears that the magic might still exist even though there are no longer nightly bonfires on the beach, nor the organized dances that brought us together in the hopes of meeting that one "true" summer love. I have come to the conclusion that it must be the overall beauty of the area alone that awakens all our senses and creates those everlasting memories.

A final note: All the names of actual persons except politicians and the author have been changed to protect the innocent and guilty alike.

.

When I was younger, I could remember anything, whether it happed or not.
        ~Mark Twain

A memory is what is left when something happens and does not completely unhappen.
        ~Edward de Bono

When time who steals our years away
Shall steal our pleasures too
The mem'ry of the past will stay
And half our joys renew
        ~Thomas Moore

Chapter I

History of Pinecrest

After all the years I spent growing up in Pinecrest, I never knew the history of the area, or how it came to be named, until I started doing research for this book. I do remember when the name was changed from Strawberry Lake to Pinecrest Lake in 1960, but why, when or how, was a mystery. I also always thought that it was called Strawberry Lake because the lake itself was shaped like a strawberry.

Much of the data I was able to collect came from a booklet written by Carl T. Fisher (1977) titled "Pinecrest, Past and

Present" and "A Place Called Pinecrest" (1999) by Herbert E. McLean, Sr. Both booklets are available from the Tuolumne County Museum and History Center in Sonora. Information from the United States Forest Service website, and "Chispa", a quarterly publication from the Tuolumne County Historical Society were also used, as well as various Internet sites.

The Miwok

The first inhabitants of the area now known as Pinecrest were the Miwok Indians, (the name Miwok is spelled many different ways, but I elected to use this spelling) who for over 9000 years lived near the snow line of the western slope of the Sierras, from Yosemite in the south, to Chico in the north.

According to "Tribes of California" by Stephen Powers (1877), north of the Stanislaus River they were known as "Miwok" (meaning men or people), and on the upper Tuolumne River, they were known as "Wakalumi" (most likely the origin of "Mokelumne").

As the snow receded each spring, the Miwok would travel eastward to Sonora Pass to barter for obsidian and other necessities with their Eastern Sierra neighbors, the Piute. One of their favorite campsites along the way was the Pinecrest area. There are several places that one can still find evidence of the Miwok in the form of acorn grinding holes in large granite boulders. One such place is across the street from the Summit Ranger Station at the "Y". Since there are no oak trees in the area, nor have any "cha'kas" (a "cha'ka" is a structure several feet high resembling a large basket with a roof in which the Miwok stored their acorns during the winter) been found, I think we can assume that the Miwok brought the acorns from their winter homes and ground them on site. Acorns were the main staple for the people, and were made into soup, mush, or bread.

Chief Fuller (1873-1958), chief of the Miwok, told a story his mother, Jenite would tell, of a skirmish between the Piute and the Miwok in the early 1800's. The Miwok, who were generally a peaceful tribe, came across a band of Piute on the meadow (which is now Pinecrest Lake). During the night, the Miwok attacked and killed most of the Piute. It is not known what sparked the massacre since the two tribes were trading partners, but the following year, the Piute responded in kind. They attacked the Miwok at Stoddard Spring, which is located along Highway 108 near Little Sweden (6 miles west of Pinecrest), killed the braves, and took the squaws and babies with them. Evidently, this was the end of the trading between the two tribes.

Early Explorers

In the early spring of 1827, Jedediah Smith made the first recorded crossing of the Sierras near the Stanislaus River. The trail the Smith party took through Pinecrest was called the West Walker Route, and is now known as the Emigrant Trail. They named the meadow "Strawberry Flat", because of the wild strawberries that grew there.

The year was 1848. James Marshall found that historic gold nugget in the tailrace of Sutter's Mill on the American River in the town of Coloma, about 8 miles north of Old Hangtown (Placerville). The next year started the biggest gold rush in history. Miners swarmed to rivers up and down the western slope of the Sierras in search of the elusive metal.

The Dams

The towns of Sonora and Columbia grew by leaps and bounds, thanks to the influx of gold miners. But in the summers, the streams dried up, causing a need for additional water for both mining and to supply the homes in the area. In 1856, The Tuolumne County Water and Power Company began building three dams for storage and flood control along the South Fork of the Stanislaus River in Strawberry Flat.

Lake Edna Dam was built on the eastern foot of today's dam. Lake Eleanor was built in the canyon ½ mile up from the present lake, and actually had two dams. Lake Gertrude, also known as the Big Dam Reservoir, was three miles further up the canyon, ½ mile south of Waterhouse Lake. It is believed these dams were named after the wives of the project foremen.

The dams were completed in 1858, and were assembled from rough-hewn timbers and stone. The timbers were dragged to the site by oxen and the use of a steam donkey (see photo on page 5), which is an engine that is used to create steam to power the winches used for hauling the logs. The Lake Edna dam remains under water even today at the toe of the present dam. Lake Gertrude dam was destroyed in the 1930's with the creation of the Emigrant Basin Wilderness area. The remains of the Lake Eleanor dams can still be seen, as well as the rusted carcass of the steam donkey a short hike up the inlet from the lake. The present dam was not constructed until 1916.

The remains of the steam donkey

The First Roads and Railway

In 1861, Tuolumne, Calaveras, and Mariposa counties began construction of a road from Sonora, over the pass to Bridgeport. Construction costs soared, so what was originally designed as a free road, became the Sonora and Mono Toll Road. The road passed right through Strawberry Flat, near what today are Camps Gold and Blue (Camp Gold and Camp Blue, near Dodge Ridge Road, are a popular summer resort, owned by the California Alumni Association of UC Berkeley). In 1863, a stagecoach station was built in the area, and it became the population center of the area.

The 1870's and 1880's brought ranchers to the area, raising sheep and cattle. The population of Strawberry Flat at that time was about 25. The area was also called Strawberry Camp.

In 1902, the Sonora and Mono Toll Road was turned over to the state because of the increasing debt incurred in its construction and maintenance. The state decided to abandon the portion that ran through Strawberry Flat, and rerouted the road down to what is now called the "Old Strawberry Road". It became designated as Highway 108, and was later re-aligned to its current location.

The Sierra Railroad made its way from Sonora to Strawberry Flat in 1905. Logging then became a big business in the area. The railroad men formed the Sugar Pine Logging Company, and its subsidiary, the Sugar Pine Railway. Logging lasted for about 25 years.

The population of central California started to expand tremendously and a cheap source of hydroelectric power was required. The three dams already in use did not have the capacity that was needed, so in 1913, the Sierra and San Francisco Power Company purchased the rights from the Tuolumne Water and Power Company to build a dam. The construction was completed in 1916, and was called the Lower Strawberry Reservoir Dam, better known as Strawberry Lake.

Strawberry Lake contains 18,300 acre-feet of water when full (one acre-foot is 325,900 gallons, which is enough to supply the average family for 18 months), has a surface area of 300 acres, is about 4 ½ miles around, and lies at an elevation of 5600 feet above sea level. The Sierra and San Francisco Power Company sold all water rights to the Pacific Gas and Electric Company in 1927. In 1983, Tuolumne County (Tuolumne Utilities District) purchased the rights from PG&E.

Building Construction Begins

In 1915, in anticipation of the construction of the new dam, a lodge was built to house the construction workers. When the dam was completed, Jim Diamond Sr. who was involved in the construction, converted the lodge into a hotel and it stood until it was demolished in 1971.

Note: One of the reasons the old lodge was torn down was that it was badly in need of repair because the management at the time allowed it to become run- down. It was determined to be structurally unsafe. A new group stepped in and informed the forest service that they would make any necessary repairs. But the forest service decided that the lodge needed to be moved back 12 feet to allow for more beach access if they were to rebuild it. The new group decided that it was cost-prohibitive and gave up. My questions: If it was so unsafe, why did it take workers over three hours to knock it down even utilizing the most modern of demolition equipment? Was more beach access needed? Currently there are only a snack bar and a fish cleaning station at that location?

In 1917, the U.S. Forest Service subdivided the surrounding area into lots, and sold "termable" leases (meaning the lease terminated annually, and had to be renewed each year). The purchasers were and are still called "permittees". Cabin construction began soon afterwards.

When the campground was constructed in the mid-1920s, Strawberry flat was converted into the Pinecrest Recreation Area, but was not officially referred to as Pinecrest until 1937.

The main Lodge has changed little since the late 40's. On the right end was the hotel lobby. The middle section contained the restaurant and bar, and upstairs were the guestrooms. The left end was Curt's Sporting Goods. Early photographs show an addition of bay windows to the side of Curt's.

The Lodge, circa 1960

A second building, to the left of the main lodge, was known as the annex. The annex consisted of the post office, beauty salon, gift shop, and grocery store. Below the grocery store was the soda fountain. As noted elsewhere in this book, the soda fountain was known for freshly made donuts. In the late 50's and early 60's, not only could you purchase donuts, ice cream sodas, and other fountain treats, but the building held an assortment of pinball machines and a jukebox. Some of the first dances were held there (see Chapter V), and later, on a sand filled dance floor outside the main building. To the left of the soda fountain was the icehouse, where campers could purchase 25 and 50-pound blocks of ice.

A second lodge, Karl's Place, was built in the 1920's by Karl De Fiebre (Karl's Ski Hill) on Lakeshore Road (Lakeshore Road is shown as "Pinecrest Lake Road" on current maps) between the current amphitheater and the campground, on land that is now the boat trailer storage area and a parking lot. Lakeshore Road is about a mile and a half long, starts where the old icehouse was located, parallels the lake, and dead ends a small private parking area provided for cabin owners. Sadly, with the exception of one building, Karl's Place burned to the ground in 1948. Up until 1948, Pinecrest had two general stores, two hotel complexes, a sports shop, a doctor, two barbers, two gas stations, a soda fountain, a bakery, a beauty shop, a gift shop, a restaurant, a coffee shop, a cocktail lounge, a post office, an icehouse, a real estate office, a firehouse, a dance pavilion, and an amphitheater.

To The Present

The only building left standing after the fire at Karl's was the gas station, and it stood until it was torn down in the late 1950s. I still remember my older brothers working there. You could fill up your bicycle tires, and get a 5-cent soda. It was also the only place to get gas east of Cold Springs (J.D. Morrison and Sons). Gone also are the original boat docks, the firehouse, and most of the original cabins on Lakeshore Road. But there are now condominiums, a modern store, sporting goods shop, post office, a gallery, a restaurant, and in place of the cabins are a couple of picnic tables, a drinking fountain, and a walkway (see Chapter III).

Sadly, none of the original commercial structures remain. There has been some speculation concerning rebuilding the lodge near it's original location, and the Department of Agriculture has stated that they will leave the discussion open for possible future consideration. Don't hold your breath.

Change is inevitable. But no matter how many man-made changes Pinecrest will endure over the next several generations, one can still sit on a blanket on the beach at night (at least until 10 P.M.) gazing into the heavens, with the lights from distant cabins shimmering across the cool waters of the lake, and the sounds of early morning campers can still be heard penetrating the dense forest blending well with the fragrant smell of the pines.

Chapter II

Camping

From March through October the fragrant Plumeria, known as Melia in Hawaiian, blossoms abundantly in Hawaii. A native flower of Central America and the Caribbean, it was named after the botanist Charles Plumier, and introduced to Hawaii in 1860. If you have ever visited Hawaii, you will know the smell. And if you return to the islands, that fragrance will trigger memories of your last visit.

Plumeria

But when you're camping, there is so much more to bring back memories of your previous experiences: the echoing through the scattered pine and fir trees of an occasional axe striking wood in preparation of the morning fire; the distant sound of a motorboat as fishermen are embarking on their early quest in anticipation of the first catch of the day; the fragrant odor and sounds of bacon sizzling in the pan and coffee brewing; the smell of smoke emanating from the lingering embers of the previous night's campfire, or the one started anew to remove the chill of the early morning air, and of course, the sometimes annoying squawking of stellar jays fighting each other over the bits of food found scattered around. These are the sounds and smells you experience before you have even opened your eyes to greet the new day or emerged from the toasty comforts of your sleeping bags. All of these, with the ever-present bouquet so typical of pine trees, combine to implant a lasting effect that you will remember long after your adventure is over and you have returned to the routine of your everyday life.

The Campground

For the most part, camping was dusty, dirty, and with several inconveniences. So what was it that fascinated people so much that they would return year after year? Sunbathing, swimming, boating, fishing, hiking, outdoor movies, dances, sitting around a roaring fire at night toasting marshmallows. Get the picture?

It may be hard now to imagine what the Pinecrest campground looked like in the 50's and 60's. There were no paved roads, no "flush" facilities, no RV's, and only a few trailers. Campers were allowed to surround their campsites with burlap or other material to instill at least a mediocre amount of privacy. You were also allowed to stay the whole summer, from Memorial Day until Labor Day, for about $5 per week.

Our typical camp, mid-1950's

The entrance hut to the campground was a small cabin in which the "ranger" lived. It had a counter where you would pay your fees, and a bulletin board where you could leave messages for friends or family to see so they would know where your campsite was. It was a big thrill to go down to the entrance and check for messages.

I remember when I was small, my parents would have "burlap" parties prior to our camping adventures. Relatives and friends would gather around long tables to sew burlap together and install metal grommets along the top edge so a rope could be threaded through them to secure the burlap between trees (It was definitely a no-no to hammer any nails into the trees). Wine, cheese, and crackers flowed abundantly at these parties. I always wondered why everyone was in such a good mood toward the end of the day.

Me, Dad and Mom (hiding behind the pots on the right).
Notice the burlap surrounding the camp.

The layout of the campground hasn't changed much. There are five "loops": Aspen, Birch, Cedar, Dogwood, and Elder, known unbelievably as A, B, C, D, and E.

Aspen, the largest, is the first loop on the right as you enter the campground. It is the closest to the cabins, but the farthest from the lake. Usually, the "older" campers stayed here, as there was more privacy, and less noise.

Birch is next, with fewer but larger sites, catering more to group camping.

As you continue counter-clockwise around the campground, Cedar is next. This was our favorite loop, and where we camped the most. Cedar also backed up to Karl's Ski Hill on Rustic Road. Karl's was just a small slope, and was used as a ski hill in the thirties and forties. You could also climb Karl's as a short cut to Twining's, now known as Pinecrest Chalet, on Dodge Ridge Road. What I never knew, nor ever imagined at the time, was that trekking up and down Karl's Ski Hill would also be the shortest route to the lot where we had to locate our cabin after we were forced to move it from next to the lake. But we shall expand on those thoughts in the next chapter.

Dogwood is the closest loop to the lake and lodge, but the drawback was that people would traipse through your campsite on the way to the beach.

Elder is the last loop before you would arrive back at the entrance. This was the least popular. It was not only the smallest, but was usually filled with tall weeds and stagnant water, and resembled a swampland. A great nesting place for mosquitoes. It was also the last to fill up.

Camping was on a first-come, first-served basis. So, on Memorial Day weekend, campers would line up along Pinecrest Road before the sun had even risen, waiting for the Ranger to open the entrance, hoping to get their favorite site.

Meadowview Campground, located on Dodge Ridge Road, is the overflow campground. It was never full in those days because of the distance to the lake. You had to load up the car with beach blankets, beach chairs, air mattresses, cooler, or whatever else you needed for the day, and drive to the lake, since it was quite a trek to walk the 2-3 miles to the lake carrying anything. Since you would need to make several trips a day to the lake area to swim, restock supplies, go to the movies or the dance (Chapter V), it was quite inconvenient.

Ahh...the fashionable camper. Jeff Foxworthy, the notable comedian, talks about inappropriate dress and what people, specifically women, should and shouldn't wear in public. In the 50's, <u>everyone</u> dressed appropriately <u>all</u> the time. Or so it would seem. One would never think of boarding an airliner dressed as people do today. Men would all wear suits, and women would all wear dresses. Travel of any kind, whether it be airplane, boat, bus, or car, would dictate that people be attired in their finest wrappings. I guess the same holds true when traveling to your campsite as noted in the photograph on the following page.

Dress well when camping?

Of course, once you had settled in, you could revert to more appropriate attire, at least until evening.

A Shower in The Woods

Camping for up to 3 months every summer was not without a few drawbacks. How does one bathe? There were no showers as there are now (pay showers are now available by the store), and you definitely could not take a bar of soap to the lake. Since necessity is the mother of invention, there must be an answer.

My father created an ingenious device allowing us to actually shower within the privacy of our camp. He took a metal 5-gallon open top container (similar to a large bucket), and had a spigot (like a shower head) with a shut-off valve welded to the center of the bottom. He then reinforced the handle at the top of the can, to which he attached a rope of about 10 feet in length. Securing another rope between two pine trees at a height of about eight feet, and installing a pulley in the center, he then threaded the first rope attached to the can handle through the pulley, and fastened it to one of the pine trees by means of a large cleat. This allowed us to lower the can in order to fill it with hot and cold water, raising it again to a height appropriate to the individual using it. I'm not really sure how he attached the cleat to the tree, but I can guess.

The next problem to overcome was the fact that the campgrounds had a dirt floor. The solution to keeping your feet clean was a raised platform constructed of teak slats, thus allowing the water to drain into a trench previously dug surrounding the proposed shower, leading away from the campsite. It was also just a simple procedure of surrounding the shower with heavy canvas supported by additional ropes for privacy. It was quite a chore to heat water on the Coleman stove, and raise and lower the bucket to fill it, but it was well worth the effort, and I'm sure everyone you came in contact with agreed.

Movies

The American Heritage dictionary describes an amphi-theater as "An oval or round structure having tiers of seats rising gradually outward from a central open space or arena" and Webster's description is "An oval or circular building with rising tiers of seats arranged about an open space and used in ancient Rome especially for contests and spectacles.

The Pinecrest amphitheater was not really oval, nor was it a building, nor was it used for contests or spectacles. It was an open-air theater with a retractable screen that showed first-run 35mm movies a few evenings a week. Of course, since it was outside, the movies didn't start until after dark. The

Forest Service did, however, have afternoon history lessons and nature presentations during the day, usually on weekends.

The first amphitheater was located in the campground. It had wooden benches set on the dirt, a screen that was stored in a long, locked box until movie time, and a fire pit. This was demolished about 1958, and a new one was built across Lakeshore Road. Complete with pavement, new wooden benches, and a screen that rose up from a storage box. You could drop by the soda fountain for popcorn, soda, or candy before heading to the amphitheater. The second or third year it was in operation, part of the projection booth (which also doubled as a ticket booth on one side) was turned into a snack bar.

Sitting on a hard wooden bench for two and a half hours could prove to be painful. You wanted to arrive early to get the best seats. A few of the seats actually had trees between them and the screen, so most veteran campers staked out their seats early by spreading blankets across them. You could (and still can) bring lawn chairs that will fit nicely over the wooden benches, and provided a back to lean against.

There were ushers with flashlights situated around the amphitheater to keep people from sneaking in to watch the movie without paying, and seldom did anyone succeed. Of course, a few shouts such as "Hey, you can't sneak in there" deterred the would-be offenders.

The amphitheater, 2005. The lake is visible through the trees.

Other Activities

So what was it that occupied your time when you didn't feel like sunbathing or swimming, hiking or adventuring, or would just rather be in the company of family and friends? Of course, today you could listen to music on your iPod, watch satellite TV or a dvd, play video games, etc., but before any of these things were invented, you occupied your time with something the youth of today has very little familiarity with: board and card games. Parcheesi, Monopoly, Careers, Rummy, Crazy-Eights, Hearts, Scrabble, Cribbage, Yahtzee, and of course poker. Whatever you could all agree upon.

Dances were also a favorite activity of the teenage set, and I have devoted an entire chapter to them (see Chapter V).

Mid-1950's entertainment

Produce delivered to your campsite

"Fruit and vegetables! Git yer fresh fruit and vegetables!" Long before Joe Carcione, the "Green Grocer" exploited the benefits of fresh veg-ah-tay-bles (sic) on San Francisco TV, as well as a regular spot on the Frank and Mike radio show on KNBR in San Francisco, these words were heard every day throughout the dirt roads of the Pinecrest campground shouted by Bob, the fruits and vegetables man.. Even though Pinecrest is not a geographically large area, nobody was really sure where Bob lived, or where he stored his vegetable truck.

Every day, Bob would slowly drive the roads of the camp-ground, stopping every few campsites to sell his fresh fruit and vegetables. Bob usually brought his daughter with him, and she handled all the finances. There was a grocery store at the lodge, but what could be more convenient than shopping for part of your evening meal just several yards away from the cook stove. Of course, as kids, we didn't care about reaping the benefits of greenery. But the fresh peaches and red, ripe, juicy watermelon left our taste buds tingling.

One day, you could no longer hear the sound of Bob's yells echoing through the pines. He wasn't that old (maybe early forties) and appeared to be in reasonably good health. There weren't any rumors of car accidents (or fruit truck accidents), and I think we just assumed he moved on. So it was speculated that he just couldn't compete with the store at the lodge.

A New Sheriff

The Tuolumne County Sheriff's Department was responsible for maintaining law and order in the Pinecrest area. The buzz around the "town" was that we were getting a new deputy sheriff. I really don't recall what happened to the previous deputy, but there was virtually no crime prevalent anyway, other than perhaps the occasional fishing pole that was noticed missing after being left in a beached boat overnight.

Riding my bicycle to the lodge one morning, a distance of perhaps 1/2-mile, I noticed a car on the main road being pulled over by, of all things, a Sheriff's car. Since this was an unusual occurrence, I stopped to watch. Perhaps I would find out who our new local deputy was. Stepping out of the sheriff's car, in a new uniform with a shiny new badge, was Bob! No hat, no gun, but with the uniform and badge, it was clearly apparent Pinecrest had it's new law enforcement "professional", but at the cost of not having fresh fruits and vegetables delivered to your campsite.

Bob was probably not one I would have chosen to defend the law, but I assumed it was a decision that was made by those with far more intelligence and insight than I. However, there <u>were</u> several newspaper articles written in 1963 describing how Bob was the first one to discover several "Bigfoot" tracks in the area His daughter still accompanied him on occasion to assist in the completion of required paperwork. I'm not quite sure why...

There were rumors that Bob really didn't care much for a few certain teens. I really can't speak for others, but I can verify that whenever any thefts, vandalism, rowdiness, or other disturbances would occur anywhere in the Pinecrest area, Bob would pay us a visit at the cabin, and question my whereabouts during the alleged events. Bob and I really never got along, and to this day I still don't understand why.

In 1971, I was living in Reno, and decided to pay a visit to the cabin. Immediately upon arriving in the area, I noticed a Sheriff's car following me. It was still behind me all the way up Dodge Ridge Road, and was there as I turned on Crestview (this was where we had moved the cabin in 1969). It pulled in the driveway right behind me. Out steps Bob! No friendly greetings were made, nor were there any pleasantries. Bob questioned me as to what I was doing there, where I had been, how long I was going to stay, and then proceeded to search my car (albeit illegally). Back then no one ever questioned the actions of law enforcement authorities. During the previous decade Bob had "escorted" me to the Sonora jail even though I was a minor, on a few occasions for some alleged teenage pranks, but I was never charged with anything. You're probably wondering about the outcome of this incident and illegal search. When Bob couldn't find any "contraband" in my vehicle, he just grumbled something, got in his car, and left.

Back to the 1960's. Seen cruising with Bob one day was a new deputy! Dressed in a newly pressed uniform, adorned with the familiar sheriff's hat, and wearing a side arm, was

Rob. Bob and Rob. Andy and Barney. What a pair to draw to. Rob...easy to describe: a very pleasant individual, although somewhat jittery, and thin as a rail.

If we didn't know better, and if Rob had played the guitar and had an Aunt Bee, it would not have been hard to assume that Barney (I mean Rob) carried his only bullet in his shirt pocket. We actually did call him Barney, but he never revealed his dissatisfaction with the "affectionate" moniker, and if it wasn't for his coke-bottle spectacles, of which we all assumed he was virtually blind without, we might have considered changing the name of the town to Mayberry Lake. I still believe he carried a bullet in his pocket.

Unlike Bob, Rob was a very even-tempered individual despite a few quirky mannerisms, and he got along well with everyone. His primary goal was to uphold law and order and he did so <u>without</u> assuming one of my friends or I was responsible for any illegalities that may have transpired. I liked Rob.

A Camping Tip

There are many guidebooks available geared towards both the new and the experienced camper. They list necessary items to bring, as well as several tips and tricks to make your camping experience more pleasurable. So I will only list one tip that can't be found in any of the guidebooks, and this is because it is such a rare incident that if it happens to anyone else, you'll probably never hear about it because of fear of humiliation.

The tip is this: Think before you load your car.

Now this tip doesn't apply to those of you who "camp" in a trailer or RV. Pinecrest in the 50's and 60's really never had the facilities for trailer camping. Most people used tents.

In order to carry enough equipment for a family of 5 for a 2-½ month camping adventure, even the family station wagon did not have the capacity capable of carrying everything that was needed. With the addition of a rack on top of the vehicle, items could be loaded, secured, and tarped in case of rain.

As I mentioned before, camping at Pinecrest was on a first-come, first-served basis. All the schools in California started their summer vacations at the same time, so in order to get the campsite you wanted, you had to arrive at the crack of dawn. This necessitated loading the car the day before, so you could get an early start.

The summer of 1959 was no different. For some unknown reason, my father had other chores to occupy his time until just after dark. However, with the absence of sunlight, he found it next to impossible to load the roof rack, and tie everything down. So he had an idea: Why not put the car in the garage, where he could see what he was doing?

I'm sure by now you're a step ahead of me… By the time he had spent hours loading all the camping gear on the roof rack, covering it all with a tarp, which he had securely tied down, the total height from the ground to the top of the load was about 9 feet! No problem, right? It wouldn't have been, except the garage entrance was only 7 feet.

Needless to say, Dad wasn't in the best of moods that morning as we left for our summer in Pinecrest.

The Family station wagon, loaded.

Who's Elmer?

Anyone who has ever camped at Pinecrest, Yosemite, or virtually any other campground in the country knows the story. My first recollection of it was at an early age, when, as dusked rolled around in the campground, you could hear someone yelling "Elmerrrrrr". Soon, another camper at another location would yell "Elmerrrrrr", and then another, and another. This would repeat itself for several minutes, every night!

So who was Elmer, and how come so many campers knew him? How come his parents allowed him to wander away from the campsite?

Then Dad yelled "Elmerrrrrr", and then my brothers followed suit. Dad explained that Elmer wasn't real, that it was just a tradition, but he didn't know how it started. At dusk every evening, someone would yell "Elmer", and that started a chain reaction.

After exhaustive research, I found that there is not much information on the history of this rather bizarre tradition. However, I did come across an explanation that the writer swears is accurate. It was in 1935, in a campground in Yosemite Valley. A little boy named Elmer did indeed walk away from his campsite, and his mother, as well as nearby campers aiding her in the search for him, called out his name. And so the tradition began. Unfortunately, Pinecrest can't claim the fame as being the originator, if this story is accurate.

There are a group of campers (30-50 or so) that camp together every year in Nebraska. They needed a name for the area is which they camped. They claim that one day, a man walked through their campsites, looking for a boy that was lost, and calling out his name. It was Elmer. They decided to name their little "town" Elmer, and they call out his name everyday at dusk. But this happened in the year 2000.

Camping comes to an end

As a youngster, I never really minded always being dirty. But as I grew older and thoughts of girls started entering my mind, I found the need to shower on more of a regular basis, and it became increasingly difficult to convince my parents of this. We had always dreamed of owning a cabin, but apparently the finances dictated otherwise. So my parents were at the point that they were just about ready to give up camping, and not just because of the shower thing. My oldest brother, Mike, had joined the Navy; my other brother, Jeff, was becoming more disinterested in camping with each passing year, and my parents weren't sure if they wanted to go through the extensive preparation required to spend the entire summer camping. A decision had to be made.

Chapter III

The Cabin

It was the summer of 1960. I was 12 years old, and had spent the last eight summers camping. A distant aunt of my mother's had passed away, and left her a modest inheritance.

I guess my mom was tired of the toil involved in 2 ½ months of cleaning dirt out of everything; of having to heat water just to wash dishes; of cooking every night on a two burner Coleman stove (kerosene fueled); of taking navy showers*; and probably the worst part, the campgrounds did not have flush toilets, to be blunt, causing at times a rather unbearable fragrance emerging from the few "chemically treated" facilities scattered throughout the campground. Taking into consideration all the fun it was to camp, it was time to try and locate to a more permanent structure in which to spend our vacations.

*A word about a "navy" shower for those of you without a military background. A "navy" shower is one whose sole purpose is to save water, since fresh water is a valuable commodity on ships and submarines, and it's also quite a chore to heat up large volumes of water in a campground. The entire procedure is as follows:

1. Turn on water
2. Get wet
4. Turn off water
5. Soap up
6. Turn on water
7. Rinse
8. Turn off water

Strawberry Lake (as it was then known) had three beaches along the western shoreline. One directly in front of the lodge, known as the hotel beach (originally, cars were allowed to park in this area, but it was soon turned into a beach), one to the right of the old boat docks, and the camper's beach, next to the first cabin on Lakeshore Road. These beaches were only a few hundred feet wide, a few hundred feet apart, and separated by pines.

The lodge is on the left, and the hotel beach is in the center. This was an old postcard. The "newer" boat dock is barely visible.

The most popular was the camper's beach. It was situated directly across the road from the campground, and crowded throughout the day as well as the nighttime hours when bonfires were still permitted. Adjacent to the camper's beach, the lakefront cabins began. The very first cabin, a two-story structure built in 1923, was separated from the beach by a natural log rail fence (which consisted of 3 foot high vertical posts set ten feet apart, and topped by a horizontal rail). It was so close to the lake you could actually sit in the front yard and fish.

We had always admired this cabin and could always picture ourselves sitting on the front porch, enhanced by the beauty of the lake. As luck would have it, there was a for sale sign in front of it. Since this was National Forest property, you could own the structure, but the land was leased with a clause allowing the government to cancel the lease at any time, which was exactly what they had planned. According to the Forest Service, the cabin would have to be moved or demolished in 3 to 4 years. That was the only reason the cabin was for sale. Because of this lease cancellation, the cabin was listed for a very reasonable amount, coincidently an amount equal to my mother's inheritance. My parent's figured that at least we could get a few years usage of the cabin in it's present location, and the government said they would provide an alternate lot onto which we could move the cabin if we so desired. We moved in that summer.

The cabin on the lake. The front porch is on the right. This picture was taken from the lake.

Here's another view of the cabin. The camper's beach is on the right, out of view.

This view is from the cabin in late summer. The lake has already receded.

No More Dirt!

Well, at least not as much. This was heaven! It had real floors that didn't have to be raked, or that wouldn't kick up dust as you walked across them. Electricity! Heat for those cold summer mornings without having to build a fire. No more carrying buckets of water from the spigot two campsites over (we actually had indoor plumbing in the cabin). No more traipsing through the campground in the middle of the night to use the facilities. No more fragrant odor from the...wait. One thing we didn't count on...There were no sewer systems, so we had an "indoor outhouse", better known as a chemical toilet. Same as in the campgrounds, but inside the cabin, and with two older brothers, well, you can just imagine. Luckily, they both quit spending their entire summers there in 1962.

The cabin had two stories, with the kitchen, bathroom, living/dining room and one bedroom on the lower floor and two bedrooms upstairs. It had been remodeled once since 1923, probably in the late 1930s, adding the front porch.

The most memorable attributes of having a cabin versus the camping experience were the shower and the clothes washer and dryer. At the dances, you could always tell the difference between the cabin owners and the campers. I'm not saying that the campers neglected personal hygiene, it was just that no showers or clothes washing facilities were available. It was quite a treat to be able to go out in the evenings well groomed.

You felt more like a "local" when you were a cabin owner, like you "belonged" to Pinecrest. Campers were more like temporary tourists.

Cabin Life

There were those few occasions that my parents found it necessary to confine me to my upstairs room. Not because I constantly defied them, but once in a while I did honestly disobey them. On occasion, Sheriff Bob would incorrectly accuse me of doing something that I was sure I didn't do, or couldn't have done because I was probably somewhere else at the time, nor did I know who could have done it because I didn't know anyone that would have done something like that. Whatever the reasons were that I ended up being grounded, I couldn't imagine spending even one night alone in my room while everyone else was having a great time.

My dad was only at the cabin on weekends, leaving my mother and me alone during the week. She was definitely not a light sleeper, and would usually fall asleep right after dark. Right outside my bedroom window was a stovepipe about 6 inches in diameter that was used as a vent for the downstairs heater. The heater was usually not turned on in the evenings, so the pipe remained cool. On more than one occasion I shimmied down the stovepipe right after dark, after checking to make sure my mom was asleep downstairs. I never did get caught, even though it was a little more difficult and noisy to climb back up.

Nocturnal bugs are prevalent in nature, and Pinecrest is no exception. The front porch had a single bare light bulb secured to the ceiling with a pull string hanging down allowing one to turn on the light. One evening as I returned home from the dance, movie, or whatever other activity I was engaged in, I realized that my mother had forgotten to turn on the porch light. As I grabbed the string, I noticed that it felt quite different than usual. It sort of squished in my hand.

When the light came on, I jumped back in disgust. It was covered in June bugs. Ugly, ugly beetles.

June bug

Before cable or satellite T.V, the only forms of media-type entertainment in Pinecrest (excluding the movies in the amphitheater, of course) was the radio or record players. The only way you could get T.V reception was to have an antenna installed on the top of a 150-foot pine tree, and then hope for the best since the nearest T.V transmitting tower was over 90 miles away. Radio stations could only be heard with extended external antennas. On rainy summer days, my mother would sit in the front room and listen to her favorite radio show with the help of an external antenna stretched along the outside of the house. Since summer lightening storms are not an un-common occurrence in the mountains, it was probably not the best of ideas to be listening to a radio with an outside antenna that could be used as a lightening rod. The inevitable hap-pened. Lightening struck the side of the house, attracted by the antenna. The whole wall went up in instantaneous flames. Luckily, they died out as fast as they appeared, and the only damage was a slightly blackened wall. From then on, the antenna was disconnected whenever the weather threatened.

We also had a telephone, but there weren't too many people that we could call. Not all cabin owners had phones, and there was no place to order pizza, but since there were so few phones around, if you did want to make a call, you only had to dial four numbers to be connected with anyone.

Cabin life was so much better than camping. You could still sleep outside if you wanted, and sit around a bonfire at night in the front yard by the lake, toasting marshmallows and making s'mores. Then you could also retire to a nice soft bed with clean sheets.

Government Intervention

Even today, I am filled with resentment toward the powers that be who decided that the cabin needed to be moved. I do not normally hold grudges, but I still think of the many more years of enjoyment that we, as well as future generations could have had; at what was possibly the most ideal location on one of the most magical of lakes in the world. Of course I was too young at the time to associate the ramifications of the lease cancellation with how it would affect the future.

This is a case of one appointed government official not only ignoring the facts, and the continued requests and pleas of several elected officials, but also, of course, the public whose best interests he was suppose to be looking out for.

Here is a synopsis of the events that led up to the end of an era, and I am naming real names, as I possess documentation that can unequivocally verify all that I am presenting:

W.L. Maxwell purchased lot #228 in the Lower Strawberry Lake Tract (our cabin on the lake) and was issued a "terminable" land permit on February 9, 1923, six years after the first permits were issued. "Terminable" meant that it was renewed annually, and that the Department of Agriculture (albeit the Forest Service) could terminate it at any time. By 1938, there were 394 summer home lots under permit. No additional summer home permits have ever been issued.

Between 1948 and 1950, all permits except one were reissued as "term" permits. Three hundred seventy seven of these permits were good for 20 years. Sixteen of them were only good for 12 years, set to expire in 1962, because in 1950, the Department of Agriculture decided that "...the demand for public recreation use at Pinecrest clearly indicated that additional beachfront and campground areas would be needed in a very few years." No studies were quoted, no figures were released, and no grounds for the "clearly indicated" statement can be found.

The cabin owners enlisted the help of Congressman John J. Mcfall, Congressman Harold T. (Bizz) Johnson, and Chairman Clifford Davis of the Select Subcommittee on Real Property Acquisition of the House Public Works Committee, and their staffs, to try and postpone the evictions because it was NOT in the best interest of the country, and no proof was ever given as to the validity of the Department of Agriculture's report.

The Congressmen worked hard, arranged several meetings, and correspondence went back and forth. They *did* manage to postpone the evictions until August of 1966. Their efforts fell short.

Orville L Freeman, the Secretary of Agriculture, would listen to no one but his own people who included Edward P.

Cliff, Chief, U.S Forest Service; Harry D. Grace, Forest Supervisor; Thomas Beard, District Ranger; and A.W. Greeley, also of the U.S Forest Service. Two bills, H.R. 954 and H.R. 3034, were pending before the House Agriculture Committee to provide for reimbursement of moving expenses which had previously been denied. However, the Department of Agriculture issued adverse reports, so the hearings were never scheduled.

In the end, the cabins along the lake up to Catfish Point were either removed or demolished at the cabin-owner's expense. I have frequented the area several times over the last 40 years, and have noticed the following: In place of our cabin are two picnic tables and a drinking fountain. I have never noticed anyone using either of them. Nor have I seen overcrowding or lack of space for picnickers, campers, or swimmers. The parking lots are hardly ever full. The only things missing are the summer homes that stood unmolested since 1923. Historical Landmarks, gone forever. The campground has also never been expanded.

To add insult to injury, in May 2003, the United States Department of Agriculture, Forest Service Division, in the "Environmental Assessment for Pinecrest Basin Management Direction of the Stanislaus National Forest, report #S039904", wrote: "The Pinecrest recreation residence/summer home tract (consisting of 639 cabins) has been designated a Heritage Resource Historic District eligible for the National Register of Historic Places. (This zone also includes the North Shore cabins.) Because of this designation, the rustic cabin-style and feeling will be maintained through specific restoration, rehabilitation and construction guidelines."

I'm not sure where they came up with the total number of cabins, since it differs from the original number of permits. It only took 40-some years and several management changes for them to realize the error of their ways.

Rubbing salt into the wound, the cabin that my parents bought in 1962, had it been allowed to remain on the lake, would now be worth approximately 133 times what they paid for it.

Chapter IV

A Routine Summer's Day

Just what constituted a routine weekday in the life of a teenager in the 1960s? During the school year, life itself was pretty much routine. Get up in the morning, shower, get dressed, eat breakfast, go to school, study hard (yeah, right), come home after school, do homework (yeah, right again), eat dinner, maybe call some friends or watch a little T.V., go to bed, sleep, and start it all over the next day.

During summer vacation, especially if you spent it in a beautiful resort area such as Pinecrest, life was anything but routine. Something new and exciting was waiting for you each day. Oh sure, there were days that unless you piqued your imagination to the fullest, you'd perhaps sit around assuming that you were bored. But even in those few and far between incidents, the boredom still surpasses the doldrums of the school year.

"How I Spent My Summer Vacation". Remember the assignment you received upon returning to school in the fall? One summer in Pinecrest would require an entire book for accurate recollections. Every day is somewhat different, and it's up to you and you alone to determine how different the day would be.

I will therefore attempt to guide you through a "routine" day in the life of a teenager in Pinecrest. First, I must preface the chronological series of events by saying that what I personally experienced may not even be close to what the average teenager, especially in this day and age (or even in the 1960's) would experience. Most teenagers were not as fortunate to have a cabin on the beach and a boat on the lake, nor an entire summer filled with other vacationing teens.

In the 60's, there were no such things as personal computers, Ipods, digital gaming devices, or any other electronic instrument designed to entertain and amuse, other than transistor radios, record players and 8-track tape players. So what you did with your day was based mostly on imagination.

At 5600 feet elevation, in the Sierra Nevada Mountains, the temperature is always slightly cool in the mornings. Sometimes it can be downright cold, but by 11 a.m. beach-goers start to arrive as the sun has finally risen high enough to begin warming the sand. One thing you need to realize is that in the mountains you are surrounded with 100-150 foot pine and fir trees. It takes awhile for the sun to achieve a sufficient enough height to actually shine unencumbered on the ground. Before that time, all you see are small rays of light filtering through the forest.

Unless you are planning a fishing excursion, which, by the way, is most successful early in the morning, there is no reason to rise before 10 a.m. However, the most important reason for not arising early is temperature related. A teenager doesn't have an abundance of summer clothes. It's too time consuming to have to change, so why not wait until it's warm enough to just put on your bathing suit? Of course, a shirt is required for breakfast, but it's off soon afterwards, at least for the guys, and I was never one to wear anything on the feet. Flip-flops, Zories, thongs (remember, in the 60's, thongs were something worn on the feet), sandals...these were reserved for "campers". You couldn't be considered a "local" unless you could show everyone that walking barefoot over pine needles, pinecone seeds, hot sand, and almost-melted asphalt didn't affect you. Besides, you'd spend so much time in and out of the water that you'd lose them anyway. You would put on sneakers (nobody called them "tennis shoes") for the dances or movies at night, but other than that, it was barefoot all day long.

Now that we have completed the parameters and prefaces, we can proceed.

10 A.M. (or there about). Get up, put on my bathing suit, which, by the way, would still be slightly damp from the previous day, but would definitely help me wake up. Throw on a shirt, and go down stairs for breakfast. After finishing a questionably nourishing meal of cereal, it's off with the shirt,

and on to the beach. Since my primary objective for the day (and everyday) was to meet girls, the first order of business was to "cruise" the beaches.

Families and hotel guests primarily frequented the beach in front of the lodge. Not interested. Hotel guests usually only stayed a couple of days, which is hardly enough time to meet someone for a "prolonged" relationship of 4-5 days. Which, by the way, is about the average length of time required to pursue romantic interests. Mostly young couples, people who for the most part were only interested in sun bathing, inhabited the middle beach. The last beach, known as the "camper's beach", was the prime candidate for "cruising". It was closest to and in plain view of the campground, so most parents felt comfortable allowing their daughters to frequent it sans supervision. It also happened to be adjacent to the cabin of the "blond-haired boy" (as I was sometimes known), so it was the most convenient of all, to my way of thinking anyway.

This practice must have been more routine for me than I thought, because I have been told that a couple of friends (girls, of course) would actually observe me cruising the beaches, and would make wagers amongst themselves as to which girl (or girls) I would stop and talk to. After an hour or so of "cruising", if no one of interest was available, it was time to move on to the next order of the day.

Moored in the water, right outside of the logged-off swimming area in front of the camper's beach, and slightly to the right of my cabin, was my boat. The majority of the boats on the lake were either small 12-foot outboards, or sailboats. My boat was a 16-footer, powered by a 70 horsepower outboard that would peak at about 30 MPH. Not that big or fast, but perfect for the lake. One of the first items I installed was an 8-track tape player, a hot new commodity. Now it was time to cruise the beaches from the water. The point of this exercise was simply to "impress" any newcomers to the beach. With the 8-track turned up to full volume, it was quite impossible not to notice the "blond-haired boy". It was also an opportunity to search the lake for anyone in one of the rental boats that wanted to go for a ride in a really cool boat.

Mid-day. Time for lunch. I could either re-moor the boat in front of the cabin, giving me the opportunity to cruise the beaches again on the way to the snack bar by the lodge, or tie up at the boat dock. It actually depended on whether or not I was successful earlier in the day. The snack bar had great cheeseburgers and snow cones, but some days there was not enough money for a purchased lunch, so it was back to the cabin for a meal.

After lunch, several options were available. I could walk the beaches again, cruise the lake in the boat, or, if the camper's beach held several prospects, I could round up a friend or two, sit on the porch of the cabin, and break out the guitars and amps. That usually attracted a small crowd.

Playing on the front porch

Around 4 or 5 in the afternoon, the beach-goers would begin to leave. Time to prepare for the evening's events.

In the 1950's we formed the Pinecrest Youth Organization, better know as the PYO, in order to create organized events for the visiting youth. On nights that a movie was not available in the amphitheater, we held dances. When the dance concluded around 11 P.M., it was time to put the jukebox away, clean up the area, take the short walk home, and prepare your thoughts for the oncoming day.

That was a typical day in the life of one teenager in Pinecrest, at least Tuesday through Saturday. The routine was quite different when you had female companionship, but it is my wish for this book to have a "G" rating, so I won't go into further detail of how days were spent when "amour" was involved.

Sundays and Mondays were a little different. Most of the campers would be packing up to leave, so the beaches would be less crowded, and most new campers would arrive on Mondays; so again, the "pickings" would be slim. Sundays and Mondays would be great for taking a hike down the river from the dam to Strawberry, or up to Cleo's Bath, or just hanging around the lodge. Maybe just drive down to Twain Harte or Sonora to buy new records for the jukebox.

Twain Harte was only an occasional hangout. It was developed in 1924 by Keturah C. Wood, and named Twain Harte for two of the most famous writers of the time, Mark Twain and Bret Harte. Long before the gold rush of 1849, the oldest landmark still in the area was a rather large piece of granite now known as "The Rock" that sat adjacent to the winter home of the Miwok Indians. Construction was started on a dam in 1927, and "The Rock" became the center of the newly created lake. A wooden arch, which is the trademark of the town, was built in 1933 and still stands by the old highway.

Twain Harte Lake is a privately owned lake with memberships available to area property owners only, so it was not a particularly inviting place to "cruise". During those few nights that we didn't hold dances, or there were no movies scheduled, we would venture down to Twain Harte for an evening of roller-skating or miniature golf. The roller skating rink was located next to the Mug drive-in (another popular hang-out), and across the street from the miniature golf course. The rink has been gone for many years, but the miniature golf course built in 1953 is still in operation by the original owners.

I think by now you can begin to realize how special Pinecrest was and still might be. Every new day would bring the possibility of meeting new people and introducing them to the wonders of the area. I cannot imagine what summers were like for the teens who were not afforded the same opportunities that we were.

Chapter V

The Dances

The first organized dances were held before I was born. According to information I have received, it was sometime in the 1940's, but the exact location is unknown. I have been told that they were held on a wooden platform, with lights strung around the perimeter.

So, I will begin with what I do know. It must have been in the mid-fifties, but I guess as one gets older, trying to pinpoint an exact date without proper documentation or the recollections of other individuals who actually experienced the events makes remembering difficult. The dances began near Lakeshore Road.

The Gas Station

Long before the present boat ramp was built on the other side of the hotel beach, the boat launching access was a dirt road off of Lakeshore about 100 yards from the icehouse. Across Lakeshore from the dirt road was a parking lot used by campers who stayed in "D" or "E" loops in the campground. There was also an area separated by rocks where you could park your boat trailer.

Site of the old gas station

At the end of the parking lot was "The Gas Station", the only building left from the fire that devastated Karl's Place (see Chapter I). Two pumps: Regular and Ethyl. An air compressor where we could inflate our bike tires, and best of all, a soda machine. Remember the old Coca-Cola machines? Shaped like a red freezer, the bottles stood upright below rails in the bottom. You could put in your nickel, raise the lid, slide your favorite bottle of "pop" over to the locking mechanism, and raise it out of the machine. Even had a built-in bottle opener on the side.

Coke anyone? Circa 1930 machine

On the right side of the gas station was a shed that housed one of the very first jukeboxes. By evening, the parking lot was empty. Not only because the people that used it went back to their campsites, but also because it was common knowledge that dances were to be held there after dark. Word-of-mouth in those days was a wonderful thing.

The PYO was formed during those days, with the appreciative help of my two older brothers, Mike and Jeff, and I continued the tradition when I was of age.

The PYO had a contribution bucket set out at the dances, and several times during the evening someone would ask for donations for new records and other expenses. They erected the lights on "The Gas Station" because they realized people couldn't see too well in the dark. Even though you didn't need lights to dance, it was nice to see whom you were dancing with, or it could prove to be quite an embarrassment the next day.

A side note on the PYO: One of the founding members was a young Forest Service ranger. An accomplished guitarist and singer, he often performed by request at the weekly meetings held in the amphitheater to the enjoyment of all. With renditions of songs such as "Superskier" and "Mountain Dew", he inspired me at the young age of 12 to learn the guitar, which became a major part of my life during my "wonder years".

The contribution bucket was left out, unguarded, each evening, and there was never a theft. Alas, I'm afraid that generally such integrity and honesty is a thing of the past. Of course, it didn't hurt that we had bouncers at each dance that kept order and made their presence known. Two of these I remember well: Mick and John. Mick was not a large individual, but with his martial arts background most people would back down from him. John was a little over 6'6" tall, and about 275 pounds. We hardly ever had any altercations of any sort, other than occasionally stopping someone from bringing alcohol to the dances (It's not legal for people under

21 to drink!). On a few occasions, teens from the San Joaquin valley would drive up just for the dances, and sometimes cause trouble.

In order for us to continue the dances, the United States Forest Service had strict regulations that we had to follow. If complaints were made about noise, we had to turn the music down. We had to end the dances at a reasonable time (usually 11-11:30), and we had to clean up the parking lot after the dances.

The Soda Fountain

In the late 50's, "The Gas Station" was torn down. The first of several brilliant moves by the U.S.F.S. They figured they needed more parking spaces for boat trailers. Need gas? Drive about 3 miles down to Strawberry or 5 miles to Cold Springs. Need auto repair? Cold Springs or 8 miles to Sierra Village, 20 miles to Twain Harte, or 31 miles down to Sonora. Gas for your boat wasn't any problem, as the boat dock had a pre-mix pump for outboards, (inboard boats were never allowed on the lake, but I do remember seeing one or two over the years). Of course, the cost for pre-mix was considerably more than the cost of plain gas and oil purchased separately that you had to mix yourself. You had to drive for a while to find plain gas. It wasn't until several years later that a new gas station was built on Pinecrest Road, about halfway between the campground entrance and the Ranger Station on Highway 108. It has been closed for several years, but is still standing.

So now what? We lost the jukebox shed and a place for the lights. Time to move the dances.

The Hotel Annex consisted of the post office, gift shop, and grocery store. Below the grocery store was the soda fountain. The soda fountain was about 1500 square feet, with a kitchen area that made fresh donuts, a long counter to sit at and sip your sodas, several pinball machines, and...a dance floor. So with the gracious approval of the proprietor, we moved the dances there.

Site of the old soda fountain

We soon outgrew the confines of the building, and desperately needed more room. I say desperately because the dances were an integral part of the teen experience at Pinecrest. Everyone looked forward to them. For parents, it was a way to kick back and relax around the campfire, knowing that their kids were in a safe environment and thoroughly enjoying themselves. For the kids, it was something that they looked forward to throughout the year. It was a place to meet "old" acquaintances, renew friendships of previous summers, and make new friends. Afterall, there was a very good possibility that you could meet that person you noticed on the beach or in a boat during the day.

To further illustrate the significance of these social functions; I recently spoke with a high school friend who told me a story, that she has never forgotten, of the one dance she had with me at Pinecrest. I'm talking about only one dance! She even remembered the song that we danced to: House of the Rising Sun! We're talking 40 years ago! Don't misunderstand me; I'm not saying that I was the memorable one. I'm just saying that one can achieve lifelong memories if the perfect situation exists.

The carefree life of a teenager: Snow cones on the white sand beaches, swimming in the clear mountain lake, spending the day with friends, and the anticipation of a summer romance that would most likely be found at the dances. We knew at the time that we could create memories for everyone if we could provide an atmosphere of enjoyment where everyone could relax and live in the moment. This is what was important at the time. Obviously, by my writing this book, by the feelings that I hope it stirs up within you, and the memories related to me by others, I know we succeeded.

On with the story...

With Forest Service approval, the PYO built a large "sand box" between the soda fountain and the icehouse as a temporary dance floor. It was about 40' by 40'. This allowed us to hold the dances outside. But you can't comfortably fit 100-200 teenagers in a sand box. So the search was on again.

Parking Lot #1

After several negotiations with the Forest Service, they allowed us to have a light post built in the original parking lot, at the rear of the lot, facing away from the campground, but the jukebox we were using belonged at the soda fountain, and we had long since gotten rid of the other jukebox since we didn't need it anymore.

So we had a large enough space to hold the dances and lights to see by. Now we just needed some music.

We moved the dances here

My father was in the wholesale food business and had a lot of contacts with retail eateries. He managed to find us a working Rockola jukebox about 10 years old in Sonora, so we borrowed a trailer and hauled it up. Since my parent's cabin was the closest to the parking lot, we stored the jukebox in the shed next to the cabin, and hauled it to the parking lot every evening that we had dances. Now we were set. We had the dance area, the lights, and the jukebox.

On several occasions, we assembled a band to play just for a little change of pace from the records. During one of these "live sets" two guys approached me and asked if they could sit in on the next set. I asked them if they were any good, and if they played with any current bands. They replied, "We're not too bad, and yea, we're with the Beach Boys." Yes, I "allowed" them to play! I never did find out if they really were Beach Boys, as no one really knew what the Beach Boys looked like in person, but they were good!

That was just mean

Teenagers sometimes give no thought as to what the reactions to their actions might be, and a harmless prank may turn into a devastating experience for others. Luckily, one such prank we played on Officer Rob that could have had led to injury or worse, had little effect except confusion. It was at a dance one evening, and Officer Rob was making his rounds across the dance floor (parking lot pavement, that is) looking for anyone that may have imbibed in the forbidden nectar (liquor, for the unaware few) when he stopped to chat with a group of teenagers. Suddenly, someone came up from behind him, stole his glasses, and ran hurriedly away across the dance floor into the woods.

The music stopped and the crowd separated as Officer Rob, with arms flailing, scurried around looking for his glasses. He really couldn't see without them! I know now, as an adult, that it was a cruel trick. It seemed funny at the time, watching an officer of the law running around helplessly while others cheered him on. We didn't allow this to continue for too long, and promptly returned his glasses to him, which, by the way, never really left the dance floor. For you see, this prank was preplanned. The youth of Pinecrest were a tight-knit group in those days. Several of us had discussed this in advance, and passed the word around as to what was going to happen. The individual that removed Officer Rob's glasses passed them to someone else as he exited the dance, they in turned passed them to someone else, etcetera, etcetera, until they were passed back to the original teen and placed in Officer Rob's pocket.

I was grounded for two weeks.

Kick sand in my face, will you?

This brings us to the first incident of harassment I can remember. It was the summer of 1964. There were two brothers that spent summers in the area. Jim and Mark. Jim was an easy going 17-year old who got along well with everybody. However, his older brother Mark had a big chip on his shoulder. Mark was about twice my size, and pretty much solid muscle, even above the shoulders. I guess Mark was slightly jealous that I had so much control over the dances, not to mention the cabin on the beach, the fast boat, and the musical ability. Never the less, Mark decided that he should have control of the jukebox.

I was sitting on the front porch of the cabin when a couple of kids came up and told me that Mark and a few of his friends were on their way over to physically remove the jukebox from my shed. I knew I couldn't stop them by myself, but I did remember that my older brother Jeff and <u>his</u> friends were in the campground. So hopping in my car, a 1952 Plymouth station wagon with the slogan "I might be slow, but I'm ahead of you" emblazoned on the back in bright orange florescent paint, I drove through the campground to round up a few of <u>my</u> friends. Including Mick and John, the bouncers!

I drove back to the cabin, alone, hoping that my friends would show up. Just then, Mark and his buddies approached the fence by the shed; it was a log fence, just low enough to jump over. He demanded, in so many words, that I open the shed and allow him to remove the jukebox. We had a few words back and forth, and I was getting a little worried since I was still alone.

Just then, two cars pulled in the driveway. It was Mick, John, and about half a dozen of the largest guys I have ever seen! They all piled out of the cars and approached us. Mick started having a few words of his own with Mark, when John, about twice as big as Mark, jumped over the fence, and informed Mark that under no circumstances was he going to remove the jukebox, now or ever. John also said that it would be most advisable that Mark and his friends leave the beach, and not return (John wasn't really that polite, but remember, this is a "G" rated book). That was the first time I had seen Mark back down from anybody, to the point that I'm sure he returned home to change his shorts.

After that, I occasionally saw Mark around, but he always went the other way, and he never did show up at any of the dances.

Parking Lot #2

We started getting complaints from the campers about the loud music, so the Forest Service told us we would have to move. Again.

Fortunately, they had just built a new parking lot across Pinecrest Road to accommodate the increased number of vacationers they expected. Yeah. Right. Another wonderful idea. So, we move again. Lock, stock, and jukebox. This new location, however, was perfect. A road and several trees stood between the dance area and the campground. Far enough away so that neither the music nor the lights would bother anyone.

At the end of the summer in 1965, we turned over the operation of the dances and jukebox to the next generation of teens of the Pinecrest Youth Organization. What happened between 1966 and 1972 is unclear to me, but I do know the dances were still operating in 1969. A new store, sporting goods shop, restaurant, and post office were opened in 1973, so I'm sure construction was underway in 1972, and since they were built on the site of the dances, 1971 may have been the last summer for the dances.

The new store. Erected on the site of the last dances.

THE END OF AN ERA

I'm going to tell you the real reason the dances came to an end. Although I can't verify the accuracy of this information, it came from a very reliable source. Since the events transpired over 30 years ago, research has been extremely difficult, so I'll just relate the story to you, and let you decide whether or not it is true.

As it was told to me: The "head honcho" of the United States Forest Service asked an employee if he would volunteer to move the jukebox because of the construction of the store. This employee, who had been with the USFS for over 30 years, agreed, and enlisted the assistance of two younger co-workers. Apparently, they tried to accomplish this task by use of a crane. Why a crane, I'm not really sure, because we used to just pick the jukebox up by hand in order to move it. Anyway, after hoisting the jukebox in the air, something malfunctioned, causing the jukebox to come tumbling down, landing on the employee and crushing his chest. He survived, but with considerable injuries. The two co-workers were not injured.

The USFS refused to pay the medical expenses incurred by the injured employee because he had "volunteered", and was on his own time when the accident occurred. They also refused to grant him retirement benefits. Here's a long-time devoted USFS employee, asked to provide a community service for the youth of Pinecrest, severely injured while performing that duty, and for all intents and purposes, not allowed to file medical claims. And to make matters worse, he was denied retirement benefits earned after 30 long years of service. This decision did not go well within the community.

One local cabin owner, whose two older children spent many summers enjoying the after-dark recreational attributes of the organized dances, and whose teenage daughter was just beginning to experience the same, was up in arms. As it was, this local cabin owner was also a very well-respected attorney.

As I have mentioned before, in a small community such as Pinecrest, word gets around very fast. It seems that the injured employee must have mentioned something about a lawsuit, because his two co-workers who witnessed the accident were immediately reassigned to parts unknown, and could not be located to testify. This infuriated the cabin owner even more. Something had to be done. The USFS had a long history of walking over anyone who disagreed with them. So the local attorney decided to represent the injured employee.

A meeting was set up with the USFS in Washington D.C., at which the cabin owner/attorney was present. At the conclusion of the meeting, the "head honcho" was terminated, and the employee not only received medical benefits and retirement benefits, but his family was well taken care of also. The attorney received no compensation except expenses, as that was all he asked for.

The story doesn't stop there. All of a sudden, the USFS paid a visit to the attorney's cabin. He was told he would now have to rake his pine needles 50 feet away from his cabin, instead of the 30 feet that had always been mandated (fire safety). He was told to remove his boat shed that had been standing for many years. He was told he had to dig his fire pit 5 feet deeper, and, he was told he would have to install a $5000 sewer system (the cabins had always had chemical toilets, or septic tanks and leech lines, which never presented a problem).

Rather than battle the USFS again, possibly fearing future retribution, the attorney sold his cabin.

That was the end of the dances at Pinecrest.

Chapter VI

The Lake

During daylight hours, the lake was the main attraction. Most activities were geared around spending the day at the lake. The campgrounds would be virtually empty.

The First Boat

It was in 1960 when my father purchased our first boat. It was a 12-foot wooden structure, which he painted all black, with a white stripe running down the middle of the deck. He named it, appropriately, "Li'l Stinker". With a 35 horsepower motor and a capacity of four people (as long as they were small people), it was a magnificent machine allowing a 12 year old to prove his manhood by expertly operating it over the subtle waves of the clear mountain lake.

The first boat, "Li'l Stinker", 1963

"Li'l Stinker" was not without it's notoriety. In 1963, Buddy Ebsen was filming the movie "Mail Order Bride" with Kier Dullea, Warren Oats, and Paul Fix in the Kennedy Meadows area, not far from Pinecrest. Taking a break from shooting, Buddy, along with the producer Richard Lyons, was enjoying the day resting peacefully on the camper's beach. This was their first visit to the lake and they were interested in taking a leisurely boat cruise. It was then they noticed the small black boat with the white stripe beached in front of the cabin adjacent to the beach, with a blond haired boy sunning on it's bow.

I guess that gave me bragging rites for the next few years, as the only one to have given Jed Clampett a tour of Pinecrest Lake, what a shame Elly May wasn't there to go along for the ride.

Me in the "Li'l Stinker" in June 1962, before we painted it black.

Time to swim

It was only the early years that I spent camping, from the age of 3 until the age of 12. During those 9 years, my memories are few. Most of the time was spent at the beach. But as hard as it may be to believe, I didn't know how to swim until the age of 12! Today, children are taught to swim at a very early age.

Before we bought the cabin, we purchased the boat. One hot sunny afternoon in 1960, while riding across the lake with Dad, he stopped the boat in the middle of the lake. I'm not sure if my father was embarrassed with my inability to swim (he was an excellent swimmer, but was always too busy to teach me) or if he just got tired of watching me trying to tread water. Turning off the engine, he looked at me and remarked, "It's time for you to learn how to swim".

My emotions were a little mixed. I wanted to learn, but it would have been nice if I had a little time to mentally prepare myself for the lesson. Besides, if I was to learn to swim, it would have, perhaps, been a little less scary if we were close to land, rather than being in the middle of the lake surrounded with nothing but water. Dad must have given this some thought though, as he never really acted without giving anything considerable thought; like loading the car to go camping.

He proceeded to stand up in the boat, grabbed me by the arms, and threw me overboard! His comment, as I was about to quickly sink, was "You'll either learn how to swim, or you'll drown". As my short life began to flash before my eyes, I gave thought to the fact that I really trusted him, so he wouldn't really let me drown. I sank a couple of feet underwater, popped right back up to the surface, and after a big gulp of air, I swam back to the boat! I learned fast. I had to. But as I became a father myself, I made sure all of my children had proper, supervised, professional swimming lessons.

The Second Boat

The next few years were all a teenage boy could hope for. In 1964, my father purchased a 16-foot fiberglass boat, a 1959 Reinell with a 70 hp Mercury outboard motor. The back was shaped like the rear end of a 1959 Chevy. The majority of the boats on the lake were fishing boats, so it was rather easy to gain the reputation of having the fastest boat. Although John, a friend who lived across the lake, might disagree. We constantly had races to determine who exactly was the fastest, but I was the loudest. He didn't have an 8-track tape player with stereo speakers.

The Reinell

It wasn't so much that I personally was a babe magnet, even though the natural bleached blond hair during the surf music era didn't hurt. Having a cabin on the beach; the fastest (sorry John) boat on the lake blaring the latest rock hits; having band practice on the front porch and running the dances three nights a week, (the jukebox we used was stored next to the cabin, and was played on occasion during the daytime), never left me wanting for female companionship. It was then that some anonymous girl gave me the nickname "Peter Pinecrest".

Flashing to the future for just a minute. From 1970 until 1980, I was living in South Lake Tahoe employed as a Pit Boss in one of the casinos. In about 1975 a new blackjack dealer, having just emerged from "21" school (all new dealers had to go to school before being allowed to deal), approached me to find out her current assignment. Her first words were, "Oh my God, you're Peter Pinecrest!"

Fishing

I spent many mornings baiting a hook with my oldest brother Mike, who as locals would tell, was one of the best fishermen on the lake. He could sit in the boat by the inlet, surrounded by other fisherman, and be the only one catching fish. He also, quite accidentally, discovered the best method of hooking catfish.

Catfish Point, located at the end of Lakeshore Road, was once just a flat, earthen protrusion about 20 feet wide, but is now covered in concrete. The shallows surrounding the point consisted mainly of tall grass, only visible above the surface when the lake level dropped. This was a perfect environment for the elusive catfish. It was also the only area of the lake in which they could be found.

My brother was not one to just drown worms for a few hours and then leave. He would prepare for dry spells by packing a lunch, just in case it took him longer than usual to catch his limit, and he would not quit until he succeeded. One morning, while fishing with Mike, luck proved not to be on our side. After throwing the common types of bait at the fish, which included salmon eggs, night crawlers, and assorted lures, our hunger overcame that of the fish. Mike retrieved his favorite sandwich from the hastily prepared lunch we had brought with us, which consisted of white bread, mayo and Velveeta cheese. An idea struck him, and he proceeded to mold a small piece of Velveeta around his hook. Thirty minutes later we had both caught our limits, albeit now we were the hungry ones, having depleted our lunch. We tried different kinds of cheese over the years, but never had as much success as with Velveeta, and it only worked on catfish.

A dear friend of mine relates a story concerning the fishing expertise of our two most (and only) respected deputy sheriffs, Bob and Rob. I'm going to include this verbatim so as not to lose anything in the translation.

The friend writes: "One morning, (Officers) Bob and Rob came to our cabin to visit (and check us out). Bob tried to convince my dad (a very good, experienced fisherman) that there was a HUGE trout in Pinecrest Lake - the granddaddy of all trout, and the only way to catch it was to put a floating shingle on the lake with a piece of hooked cheese on top of it. The trout, supposedly, was supposed to commit suicide by jumping into the air, eating the cheese and get caught on the hook. (I was there. I heard this with my own ears.) Dad did not fall for it". I might also remind you that this is the same Officer Bob that claims he found Bigfoot tracks in 1963.

Life saved

A story was related to me that on one hot summer day, some friends, Tim, Dave, Tim's sister Sarah, and I were in the boat in the middle of the lake. Tim, Dave, and I were horsing around, and as a prank, Tim threw his sister overboard. We were all laughing so hard, except Sarah, that we didn't realize that she had the breath knocked out of her and was unable to swim back to the boat! Sarah was, for all intents and purposes, drowning! Apparently, it finally became obvious to me, and I jumped in and rescued her. Sarah never made mention of the incident again, treating it like it was trivial, perhaps because of the embarrassment she thought it would cause her. I received an email from Sarah 40 years after the event, detailing the incident, and thanking me for saving her life.

Life lost

We would occasional visit the cabin in the winter, but because it was mainly for summer use and not well insulated, these visits were few. A not-so-happy incident happened during a winter visit in the mid-60's. The lake had just frozen over, and we were sitting in the cabin watching a group of high schools students from McClymonds High School in Oakland playing on the shore in the snow. A group of three students starting walking out across the lake on the ice when the ice broke, drowning all three of them in the frigid water. There was nothing we could do. When the rescue team located them and brought them up on stretchers, they walked right past our cabin carrying the teens. It was the first time I had ever seen a dead body. I will never forget the deep blue skin of those unfortunate teenagers.

Swimming in the early years

Pinecrest Lake is fed by spring runoff created by melting snow. In order to prepare the lake in anticipation of the runoff, and prevent flooding, the lake level was lowered a little at a time each year beginning, usually, in August. The rate that the lake level was dropped doesn't vary much from year to year.

Generally, the lake is full by early May. Once the spring runoff subsides, boards are added to the top of the spillway in order to maintain a level of approximately 2 feet lower than completely full. The "drawdown", or lowering of the lake level, is controlled by gates at the dam, which in turn are controlled by valves on the "tower".

Up until the late 1950's several wooden floats were anchored out from the beach, to not only provide a separation for the swimming area, but also a place people could swim to, sunbathe on, and dive off of. Since they were permanently anchored to the lake floor, as the water was let out every year, these floats would be in water that was becoming more and more shallow as the drawdown began. I remember people becoming injured towards the end of summer by hitting the bottom as they would dive off the floats. Because of this, something needed to be done. Plus the upkeep of the floats required both funding and man-hours.

Swimming floats in the 50's

People enjoying the floats

The floats are right next to shore in this photo. (I'm in the inner tube, Aug. 1952)

The solution at the time was to remove the floats and install logs chained together. It was thought that there would be virtually no upkeep on the logs, and people couldn't dive off of them and become injured. But this plan backfired, as swimmers would try and balance on the logs and fall off. The chains would break. The logs were anchored on-shore at each end, and people would inevitably trip over the anchor cables while walking along the tree line. In addition, as the water level would drop, the swimming area would become smaller and smaller until the logs were beached.

The logs replaced the floats (me on the "paddleboard")

In the summer of 1963 the logs were removed and round, white, metal buoys, approximately 3 feet in diameter were installed with a system that allowed them to be released further into the water as the lake receded. They remain to this day. Unfortunately, after the buoys were installed, fewer and fewer people would enter the water. You could swim to them, but you couldn't hold on to them, or climb up on them, so all you could do is swim back to shore.

Round buoys were installed, pictured in late August, 1963

Lake level is quite low, and the buoys are still floating. Note the lodge at the far right. Picture taken mid-1960.

The Strawberry Queen

No, the Strawberry Queen was not a beauty contest winner, although there were always many, many girls who could have claimed that title. The Strawberry Queen was actually a tour boat that operated for several years, and it was a landmark that everyone who ever frequented Pinecrest in the 1950's would remember. As a small boy my parents would take me for cruises on the Queen.

I have searched for any information concerning the Queen from every imaginable source, but have come up empty. I do have a vague recollection of it sinking, but maybe that's just my imagination. This is the only picture of the Queen I have been able to locate.

The Strawberry Queen

Bonfires

Up until 1961 or 1962, bonfires were legal on the beach, and, almost every night, you could find one on the camper's beach. There would always be a small crowd of people surrounding the fire, singing folk songs to the strumming of guitars, toasting marshmallows, or practicing mouth-to-mouth resuscitation just in case it was needed to save a victim from drowning. When the bonfires became illegal, it didn't stop the revelers for long. The fires were just moved to the other side of "the Point", near the dam, where certain law enforcement individuals could not see the flames. Whether or not those practices continue today, I am not aware. I guess one would just have to find out for themselves. They would also occasionally be held at the cabin by the camper's beach. But that's another story.

Memories of Pinecrest

Chapter VII

Assorted Tidbits

Cooling Off

Do you know the best way to cool off on hot summer days other than swimming in a lake? Work in an icehouse! Thanks to the proprietor, who also ran the soda fountain as well as the ski school at Dodge Ridge in the winter (He and his wife had ski runs named after them) I was "allowed" to cool off and make money at the same time.

The icehouse was a separate structure no larger than 12 feet by 15 feet and stood about 3 feet off the ground with a small porch. Since electricity was not available in the campground and motor homes were unheard of, the only way to keep your food from spoiling was to purchase blocks of ice, take it back to your campsite, chop it up, and put in your cooler. Ice came in 50-pound blocks that could be separated in half with expertise and skill after mastering the fine art of ice picking. Needless to say, I think many of my customers didn't receive exactly 25 pounds.

The Ice house was located here

Where Did The Money Come From?

When you're 12 years old and you've already spent all your allowance, but need more money for snow cones, pin ball machines, or an occasional snack, or maybe even gas for the boat, what do you do? Now I know you might be tempted to "borrow" money from your mother's purse, but that was dishonest, and, I was brought up to believe that honesty was an enviable attribute. We had a secret, though.

I know we weren't the only ones to make this discovery. I did read somewhere (or maybe it was a dream?) that others had found our secret.

I must describe the layout of the lodge, since that was where our secret lies. The left end was Curt's Sporting Goods. At the far right end was the hotel lobby. A covered walkway, or porch, ran from the steps next to Curt's all the way to the lobby, with an additional set of steps in the middle of the lodge to allow beach access. The porch consisted of 2" by 6" planking, built originally in 1915, and was raised about 4 feet from the ground. It was completely enclosed on all sides. Of course, wood has a tendency to rot with age, so the boards were replaced as needed. To allow for expansion and contraction due to changing climates, the boards were spaced with at least a ¼ inch gap. There was log railing across the front of the porch to prevent anyone from falling off. Many times we would sit on the railing, just to get chased off by the lodge manager.

One afternoon, before being chased off the railing, I notice a couple of people emerge from the bar. The man was counting change in his hand, and accidentally dropped some on the porch. A few of the coins proceeded to fall through the gaps in the planking, gone forever since there was no access to the area below the porch. Or so everyone thought. Of course, our thought was that he was probably not the first person to drop money through the gaps, and would probably not be the last. Time for some youthful sleuthing.

A friend and I discovered a well-hidden entrance that gave access to the area under the lodge, so off we go, looking for the treasure that lies ahead. It was difficult to crawl under the lodge to the porch, but being kids, we gave no thought to rats, black widows, or any other kinds of danger that might lie ahead. Once we reached the area below the porch, the search was on, but it wasn't hard work. We immediately started picking up coins of all denominations. They were everywhere! After about an hour, it was time to count our "booty". We had found over $100 in coins! Quite a lot of money for two 12 year olds in 1960. Apparently no one had ever searched under the porch since it's construction, and some of the coins were quite old, so, every few weeks for the next couple of years, we collected enough at least for a couple of snow cones.

I think 1964 was the last year we ever ventured under the lodge. We never did dig down through the topsoil, and the lodge was torn down in 1971. I would imagine that if one were adventurous, with the aid of a good quality metal detector, one could, to this day, search the area where the porch used to stand and not come up empty handed. There must still be a small fortune to be found with the proper tools. I do believe the forest service would frown on any digging in the area, so maybe those old coins, some perhaps dating back to the turn of the century (the 20th, of course), are lost forever.

Hiking

On an average summer day in Pinecrest, there are so many activities to keep one busy, that little time is given to the thought of adventuring out into the wilderness. Whether it be swimming, fishing, boating, cruising the beaches, spending time with that special "camper", or just hanging out around the lodge with friends, the day rapidly expires, filling one with anticipation of the evenings events. There is always that occasion, however, when most of your friends are busy, there's no one on the lake, and you're in the mood to do something a little different. Rather than just sitting around the cabin, it's time to explore.

Walking around the lake can be invigorating, but if you've done that many times it almost seems routine. The secret, however, if you did make the trip, is to circumnavigate the lake clockwise starting in front of the lodge. From Butterfly Cove at the right of the inlet, back to the beach is a mostly level trip. The only obstacle is the big rock in front of John's cabin. A few years ago I did that exact thing, only to find that the trail is now so "user friendly" that the trip is rather mundane.

In the fifties and sixties, there were certain small challenges one had to overcome that made the trip a little more adventurous. Once you navigated the slippery rocks at "The Point", and made the short trek across the dam, you had to climb the loose granite at the far side of the dam leading up to the trail. Not too much of a problem. Then came the inlet. The Boy Scouts of America had a camp on the other side of the inlet. One of their summer projects was to build a rope "monkey bridge" across the river. Before it was built, you had to traverse the inlet by jumping from slippery rock to slippery rock. Needless to say, you seldom made the trip and remained dry. The rope bridge consisted of one rope to walk on, and two ropes higher up on both sides to use as handrails; it was quite an experience for a small boy, or girl, for that matter.

Now the trail has been groomed all the way around. Easy walking by the point, steps leading up from the dam to the trail, and even the rope bridge has been replaced by a permanent structure. Then, about ¼ of the way around, is a pay telephone, and another one across the lake from it!

The bridge across the inlet

Who ya gonna call?

Back to the past. The river leading from the dam flows down to Strawberry. In the 50's and 60's, while several miles in distance, there was no real trail and the trip was downhill all the way. That only meant that when you reached

Strawberry you had to find a ride back to Pinecrest, usually by hitch hiking. Those were the days when one could hitch hike anywhere without fear. Several times before I was sixteen, I hitch hiked from Modesto to Pinecrest (about 80 miles).

Strawberry Lodge, the gas station, and the grocery store, that's Strawberry. Ken and Judy owned the lodge, which consisted of the restaurant, the bar (great place to shoot pool), hotel rooms, and small cabins behind the gas station. Since my mom worked there, I never had to pay for anything, which was great, because I seldom had any money! Anyway, you could make the trip, anytime, down the river and seldom run into another person.

Back to Pinecrest. If you were to sit on the beach and look up at the mountain peaks across the lake, to the left of the inlet, you could just barely make out a structure at the top of one of the peaks. That was Pinecrest Lookout. Used by Forest Service personnel for fire spotting, it's in a rather remote location accessible only by a dirt and gravel road. At an elevation of 8440 feet, it was originally built as a National Defense Observation Tower during WWII. It was manned from 1939 until 1973, and has since been torn down.

Pinecrest Lookout

In 1963 or 1964, 3 of us kids decided to take a jeep to the lookout. After quite a bumpy, dirty drive, we arrived and the view was absolutely outstanding. Being the adventurous youths we were, Pinecrest Lake didn't really look that far away, it <u>was</u> downhill, and, we weren't really looking forward to the drive back down. Two of us decided that since we knew the shortest distance between two points was a straight line...we thought we might just hike down to the lake.

There were no paths, and to our knowledge, hiking down from the lookout to the lake had never been done before. The way down was filled with manzanita and loose granite. The first part of the journey was pretty much uneventful. Sure, a little sliding, a few scrapes, and lots of dirt. Most of the time you couldn't really see where you were going, because the manzanita was tall, and you had to make a path between the bushes. There was, however, one steep area where you could pick up speed, and hurdle some of the low-lying bush.

What we didn't realize was that at the end of this short run, just on the other side of some bushes, was a drop off of about 100 feet. Straight down! We were neck and neck, running so fast that it was very hard to stop. Starting to hurdle the last bush, all at once we noticed the drop off. We both grabbed for the manzanita as if our life depended upon it. Which, a few seconds later, we realized it did.

Since I'm here today writing this story, you can surmise that we made it, even though we both were hanging on to the bush, dangling over the side of the cliff. We managed to climb back up, and found another route down. We were scratched, scraped, and bleeding, but still in one piece. Nothing felt better than the jump in the lake when we finally made it down.

Over two hours to drive up to the lookout, but only 30 minutes to traverse the 2000 feet down. Would we do it again? Sure, why not? Did we do it again? No we never did, nor did we ever hear of anyone else ever doing it after our story was told.

You can walk up river from the inlet to Waterhouse Lake, passing by Cleo's Bath. It's not a particularly challenging hike, but in the sixties it was inundated with rattlesnakes. We seldom made the trip, but I did have a collection of rattles back at the cabin. I guess we were particularly brave in those days, as killing a rattler, cutting off it's head (it can still bite even after it's dead), and severing the rattles as souvenirs really never affected us. We did see a bear on one trip, and actually went into it's cave. Luckily it wasn't home at the time.

That's about all the adventurous hikes we ever took. There was just no time.

And Then There Was...Romance

I am going to conclude this chapter with remembrances that mean the most to me. It is one of the main reasons for writing this book, as well as the ones that brings back the fondest memories. As you will see, it is also the one subject that sparks the most memories in others as well. This is what being a teenager in Pinecrest is all about. This is the "magic". It lasts forever...

An individual's personality can change depending upon the environment in which he is placed. The two specific environments I am referring to are school and summer vacation at Pinecrest.

During school in the 1960's, there were far less "clique" groups to which one could belong than at the present. There were the jocks, the nerds, and the "hoods". Since the first two categories were not in my favorite genre, I accordingly chose the latter. I surmised that this was the most logical avenue to pursue in order to impress the girls, and succeed in the common endeavors of adolescents.

The "hoods", they were the "cool" guys. Sports were not "cool", and education was not "cool". When you are a high school freshman, what could be "cooler" than hanging out with upper classmen?

The best illustration what "cool" was, is "American Graffiti". My two older brothers, whom I tried to emulate, went to high school with George Lucas, the film director. Of course, no one knew at the time what the future had in store for George, I'm not even sure if he was "cool" then. For those of you who don't know, George grew up in Modesto. He graduated from Downey High School in 1962, the same year as one of my brothers. There is even a statue of him at "Five Points", a spot in downtown Modesto (sort of) where 5 streets merge together. He accurately depicts what "cliques" were present in the early 60's, including what was "cool".

In 1964, you had to have "Beatle boots". These were black shoes with pointed toes and at least 1-inch heels. "Cool". Pants so tight in the legs that some even had zippers at the ankles in order to get them over your feet. "Cool". Collar-less suit coats, not the Nehru-type; those didn't come into fashion until later. All other coats and shirts had to have the center of the collar turned up. "Cool".

But in Pinecrest, during summer vacation, it wasn't necessary to be "cool". You didn't have to have a reputation as being "cool". Vacationers came from all over northern and central California, from different schools, with different attitudes, but all with one goal in mind: to have fun and meet new people. Now remember, we're talking about teenagers here. Parents, of course, had different philosophies about their vacation. As a teen, you just had to be yourself.

The stories I have included here were all sent to me by people who realize just how magical Pinecrest was (and hopefully still is). Here's a "for-instance". It was sent to me by a male reader who is now in his 50's, but epitomizes the exact situation I'm trying to describe:

"When I was small probably in the early sixties, my cousin who was about 16 used to cruise the lake for boys. One time she found a boy with a guitar. He returned to my uncle's cabin on the south shore and played the House of the Rising Sun and sang it as well. Us younger cousins were very impressed. I don't think my older cousin was uninterested either, but perhaps for different reasons."

I have only a slight recollection of this incident, but then, that was the nature of summers in Pinecrest. So much was happening, and you met so many different people, that unless you kept a journal (right...like you had time to write anything), incidents were easily forgotten.

This next story was sent to me by a long forgotten (at least on my part, but evidently not by her) acquaintance. I'll call her "Kay". Kay wrote: "You couldn't possibly be the same Pat Taylor I met up at Pinecrest the summer of 1969??? - My first love?"

Kay goes on to say how we first met, and our first evening together: "...the stars were incredible that night. We were all alone. It was my first time alone with "a boy". We sat down on one of the new benches. We kissed (my first kiss)."

Now while some of you may remember <u>your</u> first love, or your first kiss, Kay continues with such detail that I can only believe that the romantic ambiance of nights by the lake at Pinecrest enhances memories. Is this one of the reasons that Pinecrest is so special to so many of us? Perhaps.

Our last night together was, of course, at the dance, and as we parted ways, Kay writes: "I had said good-bye to you so I was very sad. My big brother...was arriving. My parents made a big deal about that, so, they didn't notice an old green car driving slowly by for one last look. (I'll NEVER forget that!)."

I admitted to Kay that I did not remember things as well as she. But as she put it: "It's O.K. that you do not remember me well. However, again, I will never ever forget you as long as I live!"

I continue...

From another reader: "I know your brothers, Jeff and Mike, in fact, Mike was my first "forever love"!"

Another reader writes: "I think the first time our family camped at Pinecrest was when I was about 11, and there was nothing particularly special about it that I could remember when my parents bought a cabin there in 1955, just before my freshman year, so I was really upset about the prospect of spending "the whole summer" THERE without my friends! I remember crying about how awful and boring it was going to be!"

"Just before Labor Day when we packed up to go home that first summer, I cried again because we had to go home! Every summer thereafter, I couldn't wait for June and Pinecrest. We reconnected year after year with friends we met there. Some, like your family, were there all summer. Others would be there for a couple of weeks and then they'd be gone until the next year."

"My older brother, Bill, would begin looking for his next girl friend a day or two before his current one left!"

"Those years we had the "Youth Center" where we could wander in from the campground or beach and meet other teens (regulars or new campers) just about anytime of the day. Dances were held there a couple nights a week but anyone who wanted to could dance whenever they had the money for the jukebox. The proprietor made these wonderful french fries. I don't remember what they were like exactly, except that they were so good. He owned a doughnut shop in San Jose, I think, and he also made delicious doughnuts. Sometimes we could special order plate-sized doughnuts that we'd use for "Birthday cakes" etc. Of course, we bought hamburgers and we also had the pleasure of Cherry, Chocolate or Lemon Cokes (not premixed but flavored by request)."

"Nearly every night of the week had something organized for the teens, either a dance or a movie at the Amphitheatre where all the teens would gather together in a group bundled in blankets against the cold either sitting on the log seats or on the ground, using the logs as back supports. They moved the location of the Amphitheatre closer to the lake after 1960 (that's probably the one you remember most)."

"The week-end dances would attract teens from the valley (Modesto or Lodi), just for the weekend and sometimes they'd cause problems because they didn't care what happened, whether the Center stayed open or not. I don't know if that was the reason it ultimately closed or not."

"Sometimes when there was a forest fire, some of the guys were hired by the forest Service to help fight the fires. Occasionally they'd be gone for a few days. We girls would mope around until our "brave men" returned and we had something to do again."

"Sometimes we'd get a group together and we'd hike out to "The Point" for an evening bond fire (sic) and party. Other times we'd drive out to Dodge Ridge for a small street dance or to watch the "submarine races"."

"Pinecrest holds so many happy memories for me, my brother and my cousins..."

I have many other stories I could tell, but I don't wish to bore you. These alone should give you a fair idea of what life was like in Pinecrest in the 50's and 60's, and for those of you that experienced it first hand, I hope I have brought back pleasant Memories of Pinecrest.

In Conclusion

The saddest part of each summer was the Labor Day weekend. On Monday, the campground would empty and most cabin owners would return to their winter homes. We usually stayed a couple more days, but Pinecrest was virtually deserted. It was a very lonely few days, but your spirits would brighten with thoughts of the next summer...in Pinecrest.

The New Pinecrest

The Pinecrest area has changed considerably since the 1930's. The devastation of Karl's Place caused by fire; the removal of some of the cabins along the lakefront; the demolition of the lodge and the annex; and campground improvements since that time have included the paving of the dirt roads and the installation of modern restrooms.

New facilities have been built including a grocery store, post office, sporting goods store, bike rental shop, cabins and townhouses, the snack bar by the beach, and the Steam Donkey Restaurant and Bar. There are also pay showers located next to the store.

The "new" marina offers motorboat rentals as well as paddleboats, kayaks, sailboats, and party-style pontoon boats. They also offer dockage by the day, week, or month if you bring your own boat. There is a 25 mph speed limit (5 mph in designated areas) so don't bring your speedboat. No water skiing allowed.

Meadowview Campground on Dodge Ridge Road has 100 spaces available on a first-come first-served basis, and three group sites that will accommodate about 200 people. Pinecrest Campground has 200 spaces with reservations required. Both campgrounds have a 14-day limit.

Even with these changes, there are still vast areas of untouched pristine beauty to be explored. Cleo's Bath and the Catfish Trail have been deemed open space, and the lake trail has been improved to allow easier access.

New generations of visitors to the Pinecrest area will still find excellent fishing, improved hiking trails, movies under the stars, swimming in the cool water, or just sunbathing on the sandy beaches.

I would still recommend visiting the area if you have never done so, or revisiting so your children and your children's children may have the opportunity to experience at least a part of what I experienced in the early years.

Pinecrest...the magical place.